SEYMOUR SIMON'S
EXTREME OCEANS

By Seymour Simon

chronicle books·san francisco

In thankful memory of Rachel Carson and her wonderful book *The Sea Around Us*, which made me realize that I wanted to become a writer.

Page 57 constitutes a continuation of the copyright page.

Library of Congress Cataloging-in-Publication Data
Simon, Seymour.
Seymour Simon's extreme oceans / Seymour Simon.
p. cm.
ISBN 978-1-4521-0833-9 (alk. paper)
1. Ocean—Juvenile literature. I. Title. Extreme Oceans
GC21.5.S59 2013
551.46—dc23
2012012590

Typeset in Bryant and Yumi.

Manufactured in China.

10 9 8 7 6 5 4 3 2 1

Chronicle Books LLC
680 Second Street, San Francisco, California 94107

www.chroniclekids.com

Table of Contents

Warm and Icy Seas

Perhaps we should have named our planet Oceans instead of Earth. We are the only planet in our solar system with liquid water on its surface.

Scientists report that there are more than 332 million cubic miles (1,386 million cubic kilometers) of water on our planet. That's a huge amount of water! The number is so large that it's difficult to even comprehend. Picture this: If all the water of the oceans was poured on top of the United States of America, the water would cover the entire country in an ocean with a depth of 90 miles (145 kilometers). The water would reach high above the lower atmosphere, all the way up to the part called the thermosphere, where some satellites orbit Earth.

There are five major oceans: the Pacific, Atlantic, Indian, Southern, and Arctic Oceans; these oceans plus many smaller seas, bays, gulfs, and straits cover 71 percent of the planet and contain 97 percent of its water. The Pacific Ocean is the largest and covers a third of Earth's surface. The Atlantic Ocean is the second largest and separates North and South America from Europe and Africa. The third largest is the Indian Ocean, located south of Asia and east of Africa. The Southern Ocean surrounds the continent of Antarctica, in the south polar region. The mostly frozen Arctic Ocean covers the north polar region.

Depending upon location, ocean water temperatures range from cold to warm. The Arctic Ocean water is so cold that a thick layer of ice covers most of the ocean. Seawater freezes at approximately 28.4°F (-2°C). As seawater freezes, the salt is forced out of the ice, making sea ice less salty than the seawater around it. This means when ocean ice melts, it is fresh enough to use as drinking water. In the spring, polar bears drink the melting water that forms in ponds on ice floes (sheets of floating ice). The Antarctic sheet of ice covering the South Pole and much of the Southern Ocean is the biggest slab of ice in the world. It is larger than the United States, Mexico, and Central America combined. In some spots, the Antarctic ice sheet is more than 3 miles (4.8 kilometers) thick. Beneath this enormous sheet of ice are mountains and fjords that

have been sculpted by the moving ice for millions of years. If the Antarctic ice sheet melted, the land under the ice would be a seabed. There is enough water in the ice sheet to feed all the rivers in the United States for approximately 17,000 years.

Warm ocean waters are found mostly in the tropics (near the equator), in the central parts of the Pacific and Atlantic Oceans and much of the Indian Ocean. The water temperatures are often higher than 68°F (20°C) and the water stays warm for most of the year. The warm ocean waters of the tropics drive

changes in Earth's climate and weather patterns. Heavy, warm, year-round rains are a feature of warm oceans and the surrounding lands. Coral reefs are able to grow in the warm waters of tropical oceans, and rain forests thrive on the nearby landmasses.

Dangerous Icebergs

Huge pieces of ice called icebergs often break away from glaciers, ice sheets, and other icebergs. Some icebergs are taller than the Statue of Liberty and can be as large as the states of Vermont or Rhode Island. Only a small part of an iceberg floats above the water. Approximately seven-eighths of the berg is hidden beneath the ocean surface, making the hidden parts of a berg dangerous for ships that travel too close. In 1912, the ocean liner *Titanic*, called "the safest ship in the world," struck a large iceberg and sank in less than three hours. More than a thousand people died in the icy waters of the North Atlantic. Today, satellites track the giant icebergs that break off melting Arctic and Antarctic ice sheets and warn ships not to sail too close.

Big Waves and Giant Tides

Imagine yourself sitting on a blanket with the breeze blowing as you watch the ocean's waves crash onto the beach. As the day goes by, the waves roll in higher and higher on the shore. Why do you have to move your blanket farther back from the water even though the waves are still the same size? The tide is coming in, bringing the water closer and closer to you. Although they are related, waves and tides are not the same thing.

The wind causes waves to form in bodies of water. When winds blow across the surface of an ocean, lake, or pond, ripples are formed. The ripples then grow into waves as the winds blow harder and longer. The size of the waves depends on several factors: wind speed, how long the wind is blowing, and the fetch—the distance that the wave travels as it forms. Ordinary big waves are caused by strong winds that blow for a long time over many miles of waters. (Tsunami waves are formed in a different way.) You can make your own tiny waves by blowing across the water in a bathtub. Blow harder to make bigger waves.

Tides are the daily rise and fall of water in oceans and large lakes. Tides are caused by the gravitational pull between Earth, the moon, and the sun. Even though the moon is smaller than the sun, it is so much closer to Earth that its pull on the water is actually stronger. As our planet rotates, ocean waters closest to the moon are pulled outward in the direction toward the moon in a traveling bulge called high tide. There is a second daily high tide on the side of Earth opposite the moon. The high tide on the opposite side of Earth happens because the ground beneath the ocean itself is being pulled toward the moon, while the ocean waters pull away from Earth because of inertia. Because of the double bulges, most ocean shores have high tides every 12 hours and 25 minutes. Midway between are the low tides of the day.

The Biggest Wind-Driven Waves

There are many places across the world where surfers go to ride big waves, including Hawaii, Australia, South Africa, and northern California. Strong winds also whip up huge waves at sea that can hammer ships in their path. In the open waters of the Atlantic and Pacific Oceans, big waves are not unusual. In March 2010, three 33-foot-high (10-meter-high) rogue waves smashed into a ten-deck-high Mediterranean cruise ship, killing two people, flooding cabins, breaking windows, and causing terrified passengers to seek help from the crew.

The Highest Tides in the World

The Bay of Fundy in eastern Canada has the highest tides in the world. Twice a day, billions of tons of water fill and empty from the bay. This is more than the combined flow of water from all the rivers in the world within that same 24-hour period. The difference between low and high tides in the bay can be more than 50 feet (15 meters). High tide comes in so quickly that ocean waters rush in at more than 10 miles (16 kilometers) an hour and cover 30 feet (9 meters) of exposed ocean floor in a minute. If you were casually walking across a large exposed seabed at low tide, you had better get going to higher grounds quickly before the water comes flooding in. You can see a tidal bore in the Bay of Fundy—a standing wave of incoming water traveling upstream against the current of the narrow bay.

BAY OF FUNDY · CANADA

Deep, Dark, and Mysterious

Imagine visiting the dark side of a strange planet way out in the galaxy. That's how different the depths of the ocean are from the familiar landscape around you.

The deep abyss of the ocean is a strange, mysterious world. It's very dark in the depths of the sea, darker than the blackest night on land. Most of the sunlight is filtered out by particles in the water and by the water itself in the first few hundred feet or hundred meters below the surface. More than 80 percent of ocean floors are deeper than 10,000 feet (3,048 meters). And many places are deeper than that. Mount Everest, the tallest land mountain, could be dropped into the 35,800-foot-deep (10,910-kilometer-deep) Challenger Deep, in the Western Pacific Ocean, and still have more than a mile of water above it.

No matter what season it is on the surface, it's always icy cold in the ocean's depths. Temperatures at the bottom of the sea range from 38°F (3.3°C) to 28°F (-2.2°C). Unlike freshwater, salt water does not freeze at 32°F (0°C) so the bottom of the ocean doesn't turn to ice.

Except in the polar oceans, there is a great temperature difference between the layer of warm water near the surface of the ocean and the cold, dense deeper waters. With the exception of communities of worms, microbes, and other organisms that live near hydrothermal vents (where heated ocean water pours up from the ocean floor into the cold surrounding water), all the life in deep ocean water has adapted to the low temperatures.

Water pressure at ocean depths is extreme. In some very deep spots, the pressure is about 16,000 pounds (7,257 kilograms) per square inch. Compare that to air pressure at sea level, which is approximately 15 pounds (6.8 kilograms) per square inch. That ocean-floor pressure is about 1,066 times higher than at sea level. It's like the weight of a heavy truck parked on an area the size of a postage stamp.

Despite the pressure, the cold, and the darkness, life still thrives down at the bottom of the ocean. Deep-sea animals have water pressure within each cell of their bodies that equals the water pressure outside and prevents them from being crushed. In much the same way, people live easily at sea level even with the air pressure around us because of the amount of pressure within each of our cells and tissues. The pressure inside us pushing outward equals the pressure outside pushing inward. Each creature is adapted to the air pressure it lives in. When deep-sea animals are brought up quickly to the surface in fishing nets, the change in pressure could make the animals explode.

Big Eyes, Red Colors

Many deep-sea fish are dark brown or red rather than the silvery colors of fish that live in surface waters. Red colors need red light to be seen. Because no red light reaches the depths of the oceans, a red fish doesn't reflect any light at all. It looks black to its enemies or to its prey and is almost invisible. Only when we shine a searchlight on a deep-sea fish can we see its true colors. Many deep-sea fish have large round eyes to admit as much light as possible so they can see in the dark waters around them. Some animals and fish that spend their lives in the mud on the ocean floor, like the fathead fish, have limited sight and hunt for food by their sense of touch or by just waiting until food wanders by.

Finding Food

Finding food is a difficult task for all deep-sea life. The food chain starts on the ocean surface with plants in the sunlit waters. Here, animals feed on the plants as well as other animals. The remains of dead and digested animals and plants drift downward through the water. Much of the debris is eaten before it reaches the bottom of the ocean floor. Some deep-sea fish have enormous mouths filled with big teeth and hinged jaws—one gulp is all they need to grab the scarce food. But most deep-sea fish are only a few inches or several centimeters long, and the largest are only a few feet (or a meter) from head to tail. Even if you could meet one of these fish on a deep ocean dive, there would be no need for you to worry about them, because they are so much smaller than you!

Undersea Mountains and Volcanoes

Most of the mountains you know about rise from the land, sometimes miles or kilometers high. You can fly over these mountains with an airplane.

But to "fly" over an undersea mountain, you would need a submarine. Undersea mountains, called seamounts, rise from the ocean floor. Seamounts are at least 3,280 feet (1,000 meters) high. That is taller than the tallest man-made structure, the Burj Khalifa skyscraper in Dubai. Some seamounts, called guyots or tablemounts, are flat-topped undersea volcanic mountains that once rose as islands above the ocean surface. Wind and waves eroded their tops, flattening them out, and they have sunk beneath the waves. Smaller undersea mountains between 3,280 and 1,640 feet (1,000 and 500 meters) are called sea knolls, and formations shorter than sea knolls are called sea hills.

A seamount that is tall enough to emerge above the water's surface is called an oceanic island. Hawaii and the Aleutian Islands, in the Pacific Ocean, were once underwater seamounts. So was Iceland, in the Atlantic Ocean. These islands started as underwater volcanoes that grew from upwellings of lava that came out of rifts or cracks in the Earth's crust beneath the ocean floor. No one knows the exact number, but scientists believe there are tens of thousands of seamounts and guyots in the oceans of the world. Few have been mapped and even fewer photographed and explored. Seamounts are usually found as single entities in the Atlantic and Indian Oceans. They tend to occur in clusters or chains in the Pacific Ocean, along the Ring of Fire (a zone of frequent earthquakes and volcanic eruptions that encircles the Pacific Ocean).

Seamounts teem with ocean life because they form a barrier to ocean currents. Nutrient-rich waters on the sea bottom are pushed upward along the slopes of the seamount into shallower waters near the surface. Seamounts have their own local tides and currents along their steep sides. Tiny animals and plants, called plankton, flourish in huge numbers in the sunlit surface waters and provide food for small prey animals. This abundance of life in turn attracts squid, octopuses, fish such as tuna and sharks, marine mammals such as

seals, and even seabirds. Down below on the slopes of the seamount, volcanic rocks provide places for suspension feeders (animals that strain floating food particles from water) such as hard and soft coral as well as animals like the brittle star. Seamounts also provide shelter and food for fish and shellfish including lobsters, crabs, snapper, and perch. Fishing ships often spread their nets in the waters above seamounts, but overfishing in the life-rich waters around these mountains has become a problem. A single seamount contains hundreds of different species of living things, many of them new to science. Overfishing might damage or destroy the entire ecology of the seamount.

The Tallest Seamount in the World

The tallest mountain in the world is the Hawaiian island of Mauna Kea. It is 33,500 feet (10,200 meters) high, measured from the depths of the Pacific Ocean floor to its peak. That is almost a mile taller than Mount Everest, which reaches 29,035 feet (8,850 meters). Much of the mountain that forms Mauna Kea is underwater, but its peak is 13,796 feet (4,206 meters) above sea level. Mauna Kea is a dormant volcano that last erupted 4,000 to 6,000 years ago.

RING OF FIRE

PACIFIC OCEAN

Stormy Seas

Imagine being caught at sea in a small ship in the middle of a monster storm that stretches for hundreds of miles in all directions. That's what happened to a fishing ship, the *Andrea Gail*, on October 30, 1991. The storm was so big that there was no way to get out. Huge waves and howling winds swamped and sank the boat. It was called the "perfect storm" because all the different factors that can make up a huge storm came together at one time and place.

Giant storms in the Atlantic are called hurricanes, but they're referred to as typhoons in the Pacific and cyclones in the Indian Ocean. These storms are born over tropical ocean waters. They usually occur in the late summer or early autumn, which happens from July to September in the Northern Hemisphere and from January to March in the Southern Hemisphere. During warm summer days, the sun heats the air and the water in the ocean near the equator. Warm, moist air rises and leaves a low-pressure system below, creating dense rain clouds and bringing air from the surrounding areas, where the pressure is higher, rushing into the area. Strong winds begin to spiral inward and upward. The growing tropical storm is fed and pushed by the prevailing wind. In the Atlantic, a tropical storm becomes a hurricane when its wind speed is more than 74 miles (119 kilometers) per hour.

Hurricanes are considered to be the world's worst storms. Although tornadoes have much stronger winds, a tornado is rarely more than a mile (1.6 kilometers) wide on the ground. But a small hurricane can be hundreds of miles or kilometers wide, and a large one is more than 1,000 miles (1,610 kilometers) across. Their size isn't the only difference. Tornadoes usually last for less than an hour, while hurricanes can last for days or even weeks.

Hurricane Katrina

When a hurricane sweeps onto shore from the ocean, it brings with it a storm surge. As a hurricane moves across the ocean, it builds up a dome of water beneath it, 12 feet (3.6 meters) high or more and hundreds of miles (hundreds of kilometers) wide, which then sweeps over the coastline as the hurricane reaches land. On August 29, 2005, a deadly hurricane named Katrina roared in over the Gulf Coast near New Orleans. The water swamped the city and nearby countryside. It caused more than 1,500 deaths and billions of dollars in damaged property. The city is still rebuilding from the effects of the storm.

Rogue Waves

Tall waves are sometimes called "rogue waves" because they were originally thought to be freak events that don't happen often. But scientists now know that these giant waves are common during hurricanes. Waves nearly 100 feet (30.5 meters) high were recorded in the Gulf of Mexico during the passage of Hurricane Ivan in 2004. That's the height of a ten-story building. The huge rogue waves that crash onto shore are caused by large hurricanes that travel across thousands of miles (thousands of kilometers) of ocean waters. Below is a computer representation of a rogue wave.

Hurricanes are given names such as Katrina, Irene, and Andrew. They are also assigned a number from 1 to 5 based on their wind speed. The strongest hurricanes and typhoons are rated 5 and the weakest receive a 1 ranking. Any storm ranked 3 or higher is a major hurricane. While hurricanes can be violent, the center or eye of a hurricane is calm, with light winds and few clouds. But if you're in the eye of a hurricane, take care! The highest winds and heaviest rains are in the eye wall, a ring of clouds closely surrounding the eye.

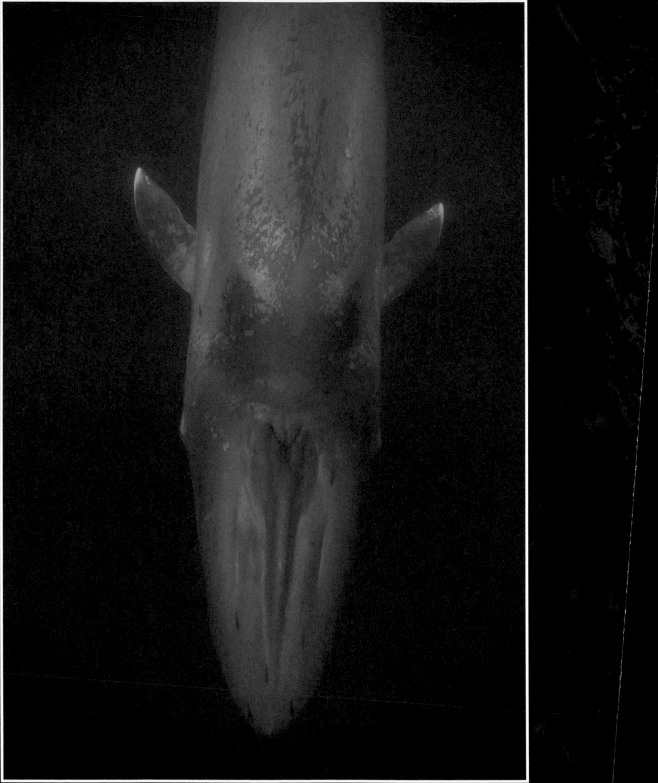

The Biggest Ocean Animals

Whales are the ocean's giants. The blue whale is the biggest animal ever known to live—even bigger than the largest dinosaurs. The largest blue whale ever measured was 110 feet (33.6 meters) long and weighed more than 150 tons (136,000 kilograms). That's about the weight of twenty-five full-grown African elephants. The tongue of a blue whale weighs as much as one elephant, and its heart is the size of a small automobile.

Blue whales live in all the oceans of the world. They migrate with the seasons, moving to warmer waters in the winter to mate and give birth and then moving to cooler waters in the summer to feed. Their exact paths are not well known, because blue whales travel in the open ocean, rather than close to the shoreline as gray whales do (gray whales migrate along Pacific shores), making them difficult to track.

Blue whales don't have teeth—they are baleen whales. Baleen is a series of overlapping plates that act like a strainer. A blue whale swims along the surface of the ocean, opens its mouth, and sucks in 100,000 pounds (45,360 kilograms) of water in one giant gulp.

Then it pushes the water through the baleen, trapping krill—tiny shrimplike animals—in its mouth so it can feed on them. An adult blue whale can eat 8,000 pounds (3,629 kilograms) of krill in a single day. That's approximately 40 *million* krill a day!

The Biggest Fish in the Sea

Blue whales are warm-blooded—they are mammals, like cats, dogs, and humans, rather than fish (which are cold-blooded). But the biggest fish in the ocean is a shark called the whale shark. A whale shark can grow to be 50 feet (15 meters) long and can weigh as much as 80,000 pounds (36,288 kilograms). It has a huge mouth and approximately 3,000 very small teeth. But the teeth are not of much use to the whale shark. It swims with its mouth wide open to collect seawater, then pushes the water out through its gills and eats the small sea animals that are trapped inside its mouth.

BELIZE

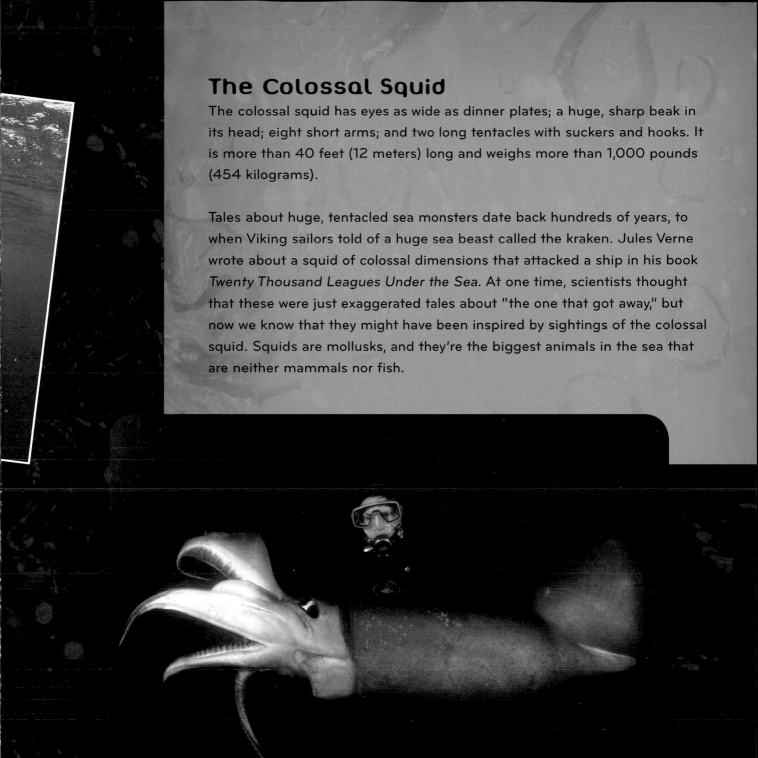

The Colossal Squid

The colossal squid has eyes as wide as dinner plates; a huge, sharp beak in its head; eight short arms; and two long tentacles with suckers and hooks. It is more than 40 feet (12 meters) long and weighs more than 1,000 pounds (454 kilograms).

Tales about huge, tentacled sea monsters date back hundreds of years, to when Viking sailors told of a huge sea beast called the kraken. Jules Verne wrote about a squid of colossal dimensions that attacked a ship in his book *Twenty Thousand Leagues Under the Sea*. At one time, scientists thought that these were just exaggerated tales about "the one that got away," but now we know that they might have been inspired by sightings of the colossal squid. Squids are mollusks, and they're the biggest animals in the sea that are neither mammals nor fish.

El Niño and La Niña

Hot or cold, up or down, El Niño and La Niña are a weather seesaw. El Niño (meaning "the little boy") and La Niña (meaning "the little girl") refer to dramatic changes in the water temperature in the tropical eastern Pacific Ocean that affect weather throughout the world.

Approximately every three to five years, the temperature of the surface waters warms up (El Niño) or cools down (La Niña) about 50° to 100°F (2.80° to 5.60°C) from the average temperatures. Together, these back-and-forth changes are called ENSO (El Niño/Southern Oscillation). ENSO causes extreme and severe weather conditions (such as floods or drought) in different parts of the United States and many other places in the world.

El Niño causes rainy weather on the western side of South America and the southeastern United States. Meanwhile, it leads to drought and wildfire conditions in the countries of the western Pacific, the northwest United States, and the Ohio Valley, along with parts of Australia and East Africa. Surprisingly, the result of El Niño is usually a quieter hurricane season in the Atlantic. El Niño lasts for approximately a year to a year and a half.

La Niña is the opposite of El Niño. La Niña usually occurs after El Niño. La Niña refers to cold conditions in the waters of the Eastern Pacific and causes opposite weather conditions around the world to those of El Niño. During a La Niña year, winters are warmer than average in the southeastern United States and cooler than average in the Northwest. It also causes an increase in the number and intensity of Atlantic hurricanes. La Niña affects the weather more strongly during winters in the United States and the Northern Hemisphere compared to El Niño.

Why Is It Called El Niño?

Hundreds of years ago, fishermen off the coast of Peru noticed that in some years the waters were very warm around Christmastime. They called that El Niño ("the little child") after the Christ child that was born during that time. The name is now used to refer to the changes in weather around the world that happen when the Eastern Pacific warms during that season.

La Niña

The whole planet experienced very strange weather in 2010 and 2011 because of La Niña. From the summer of 2010 to the spring of 2011, the United States had widespread flooding, droughts, heat waves, cold temperatures, large wildfires, and tornadoes—sometimes all at once. At least part of that was due to La Niña that developed in the Pacific Ocean during that time.

Because of La Niña, the cold water of the eastern Pacific Ocean resulted in dry weather and drought in the South and cold, wet conditions across the northern half of the United States. The sharp boundary between the cold and warm air was at least partly responsible for the heavy winter snow, spring rains, and flooding in the middle of the country. During La Niña that year, tornadoes were so severe that April 27, 2011, became one of the deadliest days of tornadoes on record in the United States, with about 320 deaths. The deadliest single tornado in the United States in the last half century occurred the following month, on May 22, 2011, destroying much of Joplin, Missouri, and killing about 150 people.

Ocean Journeys

It is springtime and a 350-pound (158-kilogram) green sea turtle swims steadily in the vast open waters of the South Atlantic Ocean.

She's heading for Ascension Island, a speck of land just 5 miles (8 kilometers) wide, more than 1,300 miles (2,092 kilometers) away from the coast of Brazil, where she has been feeding for several years. Once she arrives on the island, the giant turtle will hollow out a hole on the sandy beach with her flippers, lay dozens of eggs, and cover them with sand. After a few weeks of warm sun, the hard-shelled eggs hatch and the young turtles run as fast as they can down the beach to the sea. The hatchlings are threatened on all sides by birds, crabs, and other animals. Only a few escape the onslaught and grow to become adults.

By June, the beaches on Ascension Island are deserted. The turtles are swimming back to their feeding waters more than a thousand miles away. And sure enough, several years later, adult females begin to return to the same beach on Ascension Island from which they left.

A leatherback sea turtle's journey is even longer. One leatherback turtle was tagged and then tracked by satellite for 647 days as it traveled from its warm nesting beach on Papua, Indonesia, to its cold-water feeding grounds off the coast of Oregon. This journey of more than 12,000 miles (19,312 kilometers) is the longest migration known for any sea animal. No one has discovered how sea turtles find the way for their long journeys, which take them hundreds and thousands of miles or kilometers. Scientists believe that, like sailors of long ago, the turtles use the positions of the stars, sun, and moon to guide them. When the turtles get close to the shores where they were hatched, they may use their sense of smell to return to the same beach. Whatever the explanation, sea turtles do return to the exact same beach from which they were hatched.

PAPUA • INDONESIA

Why Take the Trip?

Whales, seals, salmon, eels, lobsters, and many other sea creatures migrate to breed and feed seasonally. Some travel hundreds or thousands of miles or kilometers, while others travel much shorter distances. Animals migrate for two reasons: to find a favorable place to mate and reproduce and because of seasonal changes in food supplies (animals regularly travel to where more food is available).

Journeys Up and Down

Even tiny sea animals called zooplankton go on journeys, but their journeys are up and down, as if on an elevator. In polar ocean waters, darkness lasts for several months of the year. The zooplankton may move to the surface of the ocean in the summer and to deeper waters during the winter. In temperate and tropical oceans, zooplankton move up to surface waters at night and to deeper waters during daylight. These "elevator" zooplankton travel up and down a thousand feet (300 meters) or more every day of the year. These daily journeys help zooplankton avoid fish that prey on them near the surface during the day, as well as nocturnal predators at the sea bottom that use other senses to hunt in the dark of night.

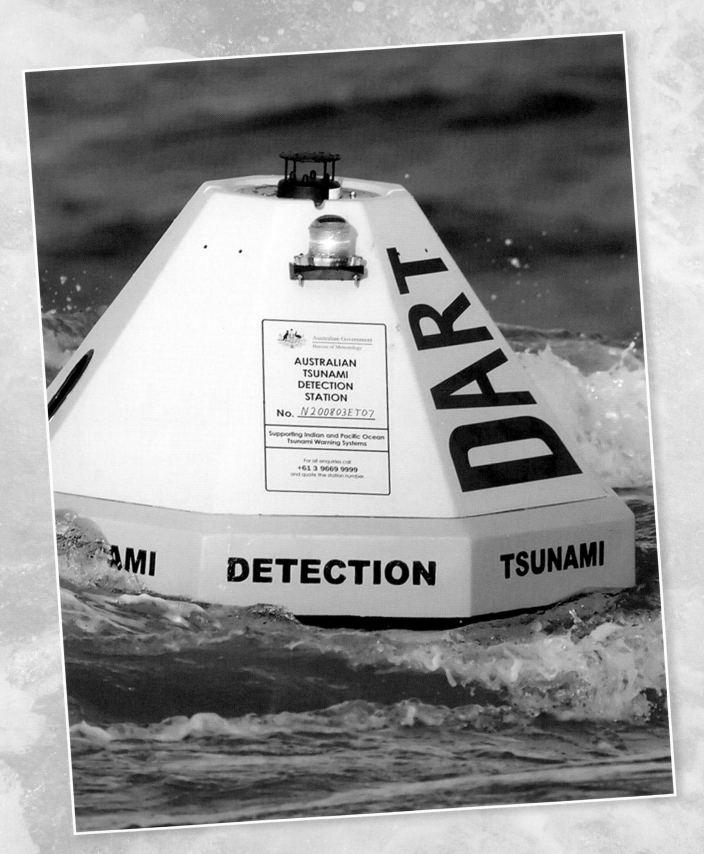

Dangerous Tsunamis

Tsunamis are not the kind of waves we see coming in or going out each day at the beach. Tsunamis are caused by violent earthquakes or volcanic eruptions. Not all earthquakes generate tsunamis—the earthquake has to be powerful in magnitude, cover a large area, and be underneath or near the ocean. Such an earthquake can generate a wave that travels across deep ocean waters at speeds up to 600 miles (965 kilometers) per hour—faster than a commercial jet plane.

In the open ocean, a tsunami wave may be barely noticeable, a foot high (30 centimeters) or less. In the ocean there is space for the energy in a tsunami to spread far and wide. Tsunami waves are often 60 miles (100 kilometers) or more apart, and the time between the wave crests is also very great in the ocean, ranging from five or ten minutes to an hour apart. But when tsunami waves reach shallow coastal waters, the waves slow down, the crests get closer and closer together, and they begin to grow higher and higher. The water can pile up into a towering wall of destruction, 100 feet (30 meters) or more in height, and hit with the force of a locomotive. The first wave of a

tsunami may not be the largest. The danger can last for hours, and a breaking tsunami wave can move faster than a person can run.

The power of tsunamis can be enormous. Ships and houses, along with large rocks and other debris, can be carried far inland from the shore and leave a path of destruction. Tsunamis can travel for miles up rivers and streams.

They can occur at any time, day or night. The wave can wrap around shorelines, so that it's just as dangerous on coasts not facing the earthquake that caused the tsunami.

What You Should Know

As dangerous as tsunamis are, they don't happen very often. Tsunamis can occur in any of the world's oceans, but they are more likely on shorelines around the Pacific Ring of Fire, because of the many large earthquakes that happen there. That doesn't mean you shouldn't go to enjoy the ocean. Just be sure you know the signs of a possible tsunami:

- The water pulls out to sea, exposing ocean floor.
- You hear a train-like roar coming toward you.
- When a tsunami hits, the ground shakes beneath your feet.

Tsunamis generated in distant places far from land usually give scientists enough advance warning to alert people to move to higher ground. High, multistory concrete office buildings and hotels are safer than most homes and small buildings near the shore. The upper floors may be safer places to go if you cannot move quickly inland.

Great Barrier Reef

The Great Barrier Reef stretches for approximately 1,200 miles (1,930 kilometers) off the northeastern coast of Australia. The Great Barrier Reef is big enough to be seen from space satellites, but the huge structure is made of countless tiny animals, each approximately the size of a pinhead, called coral polyps.

A coral polyp is a sea animal that is mostly a stomach and a mouth surrounded by retractable, stinging tentacles. A hard limestone shell protects the polyp. In shallow, warm seas, the polyps grow and multiply, slowly building colonies called coral reefs on the underlying sand and rock. Green plants called algae help bind the coral, sand, and rock together. Colonies of coral polyps grow in a variety of shapes with names such as brain coral, staghorn coral, and table coral. Living coral is an assortment of different colors such as green or red, but when coral dies it bleaches white and becomes hard. The Great Barrier Reef has more than 400 different kinds of coral. The huge reef is made up of 3,000 smaller reefs and coral islands.

The Great Barrier Reef is home to a huge variety of sea animals and plants. As many as 1,600 different kinds of fish live in the waters of the reef. Some are huge, such as visiting whale sharks. Many of the reef's fish are brightly colored, like the anemone fish (more commonly known as a clown fish) and the butterfly fish. Sea snakes, sea turtles, sea birds, whales, dolphins, and porpoises also live in or visit the Great Barrier Reef. Giant clams on the reef may grow to more than 3 feet (1 meter) wide and are the largest clams in the world. All kinds of shellfish abound, including nudibranchs, a kind of sea snail that loses its shell as it passes out of the larval stage. One of the very colorful creatures that scientists found living on the coral in the Great Barrier Reef was what they called the Christmas tree worm. The "branches" of the tree are the structures the worm uses to breathe and feed. The worm lives in a tube and can withdraw its treelike branches if threatened.

THE GREAT BARRIER REEF

AUSTRALIA

Coral Reefs Under Attack

Some portions of the reef are being destroyed by the crown-of-thorns starfish. This starfish is approximately 20 inches (50 centimeters) across and has ten to twenty arms covered in long, slightly venomous spines. These stars feed on living coral by turning their stomachs inside out through their mouths and enclosing and digesting the coral's living polyps. Patches of white coral skeletons in the Great Barrier Reef are one sign that the crown-of-thorns has been feeding in the area.

Warming ocean temperatures and the run-off of fertilizers, pesticides, and sediments into the surrounding sea are also affecting the reef. Reefs can recover after a bad bleaching year (when a lot of coral is killed and turns white), but the long-term outlook for the world's coral reefs is not good.

The Census of Marine Life

The Census of Marine Life is an international effort by almost 3,000 scientists to answer these questions: What lives, has lived, or will live in the world's oceans? These scientists have searched for years gathering data in the oceans from the North Pole to the South Pole and from the surface of the ocean to the sea bottom about ocean life, from the smallest bacteria to the largest whales. The scientists think that there may be half a million to ten million ocean creatures yet to be discovered.

Dangerous Sea Animals

Sharks are the best known of all the dangerous sea animals, with good reason. Sharks are killing machines with powerful jaws and rows of razor-sharp teeth. Some sharks bite with a force many times stronger than a person's bite, enough to cut through a piece of steel. Books, the Internet, television, and movies often tell stories of sharks on the attack.

But the truth is most sharks are harmless to humans. Of the approximately 400 known kinds of sharks, only a dozen are a serious threat. The most dangerous are the great white shark, the tiger shark, and the bull shark. There are fewer than 100 shark attacks reported each year, and most people survive the encounter.

In tropical oceans, saltwater crocodiles are a threat. A saltwater crocodile can reach a length of 20 feet (6 meters), has large, powerful jaws, can swim fast, and can run on land. In Australian ocean waters, crocodile attacks are not uncommon.

Poisonous sea animals are considered even more dangerous than sharks and crocodiles. Poisonous fish that live in Australian waters, such as the lionfish and the stonefish, are bad enough, but box jellyfish are even more dangerous. A box jellyfish is aptly named, as it looks like a box. It is as big as a basketball, with approximately 15 long tentacles hanging from each of its bottom four boxlike corners. The tentacles are covered with thousands of stinging cells, each with a micro harpoon and a poison sac. The cells are triggered into action when the tentacles touch a fish, mollusk, or human. When a person accidentally gets touched and stung by a box jellyfish's tentacles, they can die from heart failure within minutes. Poisonous jellyfish kill more humans than sharks and crocodiles combined.

Beware of Irukandjis!

Irukandjis (ear-uh-CAN-jeez) are poisonous jellyfish about the size of a peanut and have only one tentacle at each corner of their boxlike bodies. These jellies can easily pass through nets that Australians put up to keep big box jellyfish away from swimming beaches. The sting from one of these tiny jellyfish is not bad. But 20 to 30 minutes later, victims of the sting endure agonizing pain and cramps that lasts for hours. Most people don't die from the sting, but the experience is terrifying.

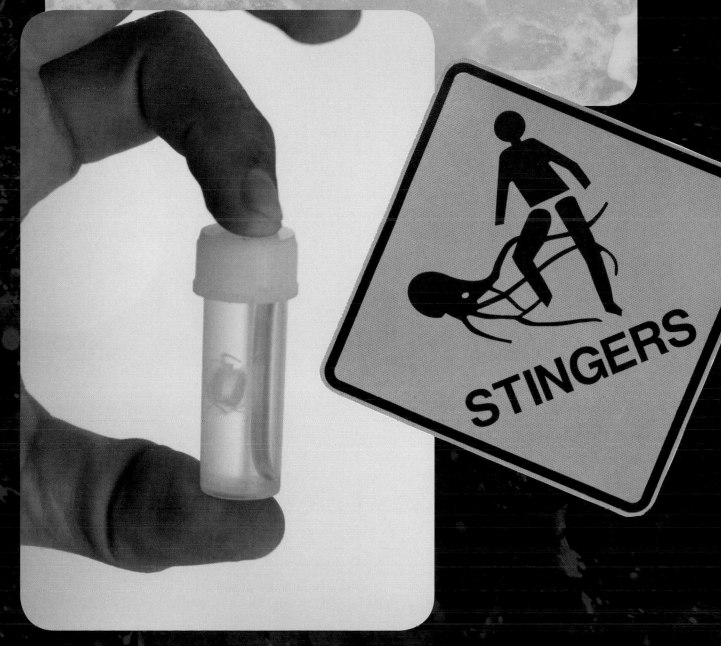

STINGERS

Climate Change

Air temperatures vary from year to year, rising and falling from causes like El Niño making air temperatures warmer or a large volcanic explosion creating a huge cloud of dust that makes air temperatures cooler for a long period of time.

But these events, in time, cancel each other out. To understand whether Earth has been warming up for at least the past hundred years, scientists often look to the oceans for answers. The world's oceans are a huge reservoir of water with a stable temperature. Oceans are slow to heat up and slow to cool down. Scientists have studied ocean temperature records for several decades. Even though there is a large amount of uncertainty in looking at the data, most scientists agree that there are clear signs of warming in the oceans during the time they collected data, over the last twenty years.

As water warms, it expands. So as oceans warm, they become bigger. The rise at sea level is gradual and may vary from one year to another, but over time there has been a measurable rise. One hundred years ago, sea levels were rising approx-imately 0.04 inch (1 millimeter) per year. Fifty years ago, it was 0.08 inch (2 millimeters) per year. Now the water level is rising about 0.12 inch (3 millimeters) per year. That's three times as fast as at the start of the last century. The Arctic Ocean is frozen over the entire year, but the amount of sea ice always gets larger in the winter and smaller in the summer. In September, sea ice is at its minimum for the year. September sea ice has been decreasing at a rate of approximately 11.5 percent per decade since 1979. Studying changes in the oceans is an important way of understanding any climate change and to under-stand what is happening to our planet.

2005

1932

BANGLADESH

What If Sea Levels Continue to Rise?

Some scientists believe that by the end of the twenty-second century, sea levels may rise as much as 2 feet (61 centimeters). Ten percent of the world's population lives in coastal areas in danger of being flooded. The rising sea level would cause flooding during small storms, and when hurricanes hit the coast, the flooding would be catastrophic. In the future, people living in low-lying coastal places may have to move to higher ground or build giant sea walls to hold back the ocean.

Index

Photo Credits

Permission to use the following photographs is gratefully acknowledged:

Cover: (wave background) © Feng Yu/Shutterstock, (Hurricane Katrina from space) © Matt Trommer/Shutterstock, (seal) © Simone Janssen/Shutterstock, (surfer) © EpicStockMedia/Shutterstock, (Shortfin Mako Shark) © Andy Murch/Elasmodiver.com, (Polar Bear) © J. L. Klein & M. L. Hubert/Photo Researchers, Inc., (reef in Raja Ampat, Indonesia) © FAUP/Shutterstock, (Atlantic iceberg) © Sergej Khakimullin/Shutterstock, (coast guard cutter) © Eric Geveart/Shutterstock; p. 4–7, 13–15, 21–23, 25–27, 33–35, 41–43, 45–47, 51, 53–57 (wave background) © Feng Yu/Shutterstock; p. 8 (Atlantic iceberg) © Sergej Khakimullin/Shutterstock; p. 9–11, 37–39 (splash background) © saiva_l/Shutterstock; p. 10 (Perito Moreno Glacier) © Pablo H. Caridad/Shutterstock, (plane/South Pole stamp) © astudio/Shutterstock; p. 11, 17–19, 23, 26–27, 29–31, 34–35, 43, 47, 49–51, 55 (water background) © maga/Shutterstock; p. 11 (ship in Antarctic) © Dmytro Pylypenko/Shutterstock; p. 12 (wave breaking offshore) © EpicStockMedia/Shutterstock; p. 14 (surfer) © EpicStockMedia/Shutterstock; p. 15 (Canada stamp) © squareologo/Shutterstock, (crashing wave) © Zacarias Pereira da Mata/Shutterstock, (Bay of Fundy low tide) © V. J. Matthew/123RF, (Bay of Fundy high tide) © Graça Victoria/123RF; p. 16 (strange creature: Cnidarian) Courtesy of Hidden Ocean 2005 Expedition: NOAA Office of Ocean Exploration, (SCUBA diver) © Shane Gross/Shutterstock; p. 18 (siphonophore "dandelion") Courtesy of NOAA Okeanos Explorer Program, Galapagos Rift Expedition 2011; p.18–19 (Deep Sea Lizardfish) © Peter Batson, DeepSeaPhotography.com; p. 19 (fish stamp) © astudio/Shutterstock, (Beryx Decadactylus) © Dr. Ken Sulak, USGS Life on the Edge 2004 Expedition: NOAA Office of Ocean Exploration; p. 20 (eels) © Image courtesy of Vailulu'u 2005 Exploration, NOAA-OE, (moon) © granat/Shutterstock; p. 22 (seal) © Simone Janssen/Shutterstock; p. 22–23 (White Chimneys, Champagne Vent Site) Courtesy of Pacific Ring of Fire 2004 Expedition, NOAA Office of Ocean Exploration, Dr. Bob Embley, NOAA PMEL, Chief Scientist; p. 23 (sunset on Mauna Kea, Hawaii) © Galyna Andrushko/Shutterstock, (retro stamp) © ShEd Artworks/Shutterstock; p. 24 (stormy seas) © andrej pol/Shutterstock; p. 26 (New Orleans stamp) © Oxlock/Shutterstock, (fleur de lys in stamp) © Alex Kalmbach/Shutterstock, (Hurricane Katrina from space) © Matt Trommer/Shutterstock, (Hurricane Katrina flooding) © Caitlin Mirra/Shutterstock; p. 27 (wave art) © Dr. Eric J. Heller, (coast guard cutter) © Eric Geveart/Shutterstock; p. 28 (blue whale) © Minden Pictures/SuperStock; p. 30 (Whale Shark) © Valerie Taylor/ardea.com, (Belize stamp) © ShEd Artworks/Shutterstock, (Belize silhouette) © visioner/Shutterstock, (fish silhouette) © Thumbelina/Shutterstock; p. 30–31 (Whale Shark) © paul cowell/Shutterstock; p. 31 (Scuba Diver with Jumbo Squid) © Franco Banfi/Getty Images; p. 32 (wildfire) © akiyoko/Shutterstock; p. 34 (Tuscaloosa tornado damage) © NASA/SPORT, (Hurricane Ivan Map) Courtesy NOAA; p. 35 (Missouri stamp) © squarelogo/Shutterstock, (La Nina: Joplin, MO) © Dustie/Shutterstock; p. 36 (turtle) © D. Parer & E. Parer-Cook/ardea.com; p. 38, (sea turtle stamp) © Sim Kay Seng/Shutterstock; p. 38 (sea turtle hatchlings) © Jean Paul Ferrero/ardea.com; p. 39 (Lobster Migration) © Doug Perrine/SeaPics.com, (Zooplankton) © Dario Sabljak/Shutterstock, (lobster) © littlesam/Shutterstock; p. 40 (tsunami warning equipment) © AP Images; p. 42 (tsunami hazard zone sign) © J.D.S./Shutterstock, (tsunami evacuation route sign) © think-4photop/Shutterstock; p. 43 (tall building left standing) © Rex Features via AP Images, (3 tsunami images) Courtesy of the Iwate Prefectural Museum/AP Images; p. 44 (aerial shot of extensive coastal reefs) © tororo reaction/Shutterstock; p. 46 (Australia stamp) © astudio/Shutterstock, (reef in Raja Ampat, Indonesia) © FAUP/Shutterstock; p. 47 (Crown of Thorns Starfish) © iDive-Deep/Shutterstock, (Crossota) © Kevin Raskoff, Hidden Ocean 2005 Expedition: NOAA Office of Ocean Exploration; p. 48 (Saltwater Crocodile) © Jean Paul Ferrero/ardea.com; p. 50 (Porbeagle Shark) © Andy Murch/Elasmodiver.com, (Shortfin Mako Shark) © Andy Murch/Elasmodiver.com; p. 51 (vial with Irukandji jellyfish) © GondwanaGirl, (warning sign) © Johan Larson/Shutterstock; p. 52 (iceberg with penguins) © Andrey Pavlov/Shutterstock; p. 54 (Boulder Glacier: 1932) © T.J. Hileman, courtesy of Glacier National Park Archives, (Boulder Glacier: 2005) © Greg Pederson, courtesy of USGS; p. 55 (Polar Bear) © J. L. Klein & M. L. Hubert /Photo Researchers, Inc., (Bangladeshi villagers) © AP Photo/Pavel Rahman.